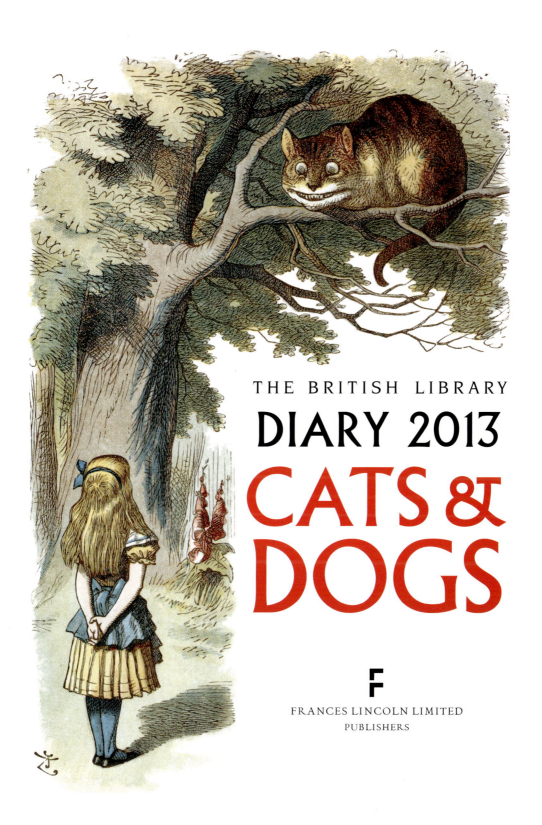

THE BRITISH LIBRARY

# DIARY 2013

# CATS &
# DOGS

**F**

FRANCES LINCOLN LIMITED
PUBLISHERS

Frances Lincoln Limited
4 Torriano Mews
Torriano Avenue
London NW5 2RZ
www.franceslincoln.com

*The British Library Desk Diary 2013*
Copyright © Frances Lincoln Limited 2012
Images and text © The British Library 2012

Astronomical information © Crown Copyright.
Reproduced by permission of the Controller of Her
Majesty's Stationery Office and the UK Hydrographic
Office (www.ukho.gov.uk)

A catalogue record for this book is available
from the British Library

ISBN: 978-0-7112-3315-7

Printed and bound in China

1 2 3 4 5 6 7 8 9

FRONT COVER: Illustration by Cecil Aldin from *Jack & Jill* by
May Byron, 1914. [1874.f.19]
BACK COVER: 'The Owl and the Pussycat', illustration from
*The Nonsense Book* by Edward Lear, 1910. [12812.bb.26]
TITLE PAGE: The Cheshire Cat from Lewis Carroll's *Nursery Alice*.
Illustration by Sir John Tenniel, 1890. [Cup.410.g.74]
RIGHT: 'The Bremen Town Musicians', from *The Fairy Tales
of the Brothers Grimm*, translated by Mrs Edgar Lucas, 1909.
Illustration by Arthur Rackham. [K.T.C.42.b.10]
FRONT ENDPAPERS: Title page illustration from *The Twins* by
Cecil Aldin, 1910. [1874.b.52]
BACK ENDPAPERS: Illustration from *The Twins* by Cecil Aldin,
1910. [1874.b.52]
INTRODUCTION: 'The Clever Cats. London Pavilion, Piccadilly'.
Poster, 1888. [Evanion 296]

# ∾ 2013 ∾

## JANUARY
| M | T | W | T | F | S | S |
|---|---|---|---|---|---|---|
|   | 1 | 2 | 3 | 4 | 5 | 6 |
| 7 | 8 | 9 | 10 | 11 | 12 | 13 |
| 14 | 15 | 16 | 17 | 18 | 19 | 20 |
| 21 | 22 | 23 | 24 | 25 | 26 | 27 |
| 28 | 29 | 30 | 31 |   |   |   |

## FEBRUARY
| M | T | W | T | F | S | S |
|---|---|---|---|---|---|---|
|   |   |   |   | 1 | 2 | 3 |
| 4 | 5 | 6 | 7 | 8 | 9 | 10 |
| 11 | 12 | 13 | 14 | 15 | 16 | 17 |
| 18 | 19 | 20 | 21 | 22 | 23 | 24 |
| 25 | 26 | 27 | 28 |   |   |   |

## MARCH
| M | T | W | T | F | S | S |
|---|---|---|---|---|---|---|
|   |   |   |   | 1 | 2 | 3 |
| 4 | 5 | 6 | 7 | 8 | 9 | 10 |
| 11 | 12 | 13 | 14 | 15 | 16 | 17 |
| 18 | 19 | 20 | 21 | 22 | 23 | 24 |
| 25 | 26 | 27 | 28 | 29 | 30 | 31 |

## APRIL
| M | T | W | T | F | S | S |
|---|---|---|---|---|---|---|
| 1 | 2 | 3 | 4 | 5 | 6 | 7 |
| 8 | 9 | 10 | 11 | 12 | 13 | 14 |
| 15 | 16 | 17 | 18 | 19 | 20 | 21 |
| 22 | 23 | 24 | 25 | 26 | 27 | 28 |
| 29 | 30 |   |   |   |   |   |

## MAY
| M | T | W | T | F | S | S |
|---|---|---|---|---|---|---|
|   | 1 | 2 | 3 | 4 | 5 |   |
| 6 | 7 | 8 | 9 | 10 | 11 | 12 |
| 13 | 14 | 15 | 16 | 17 | 18 | 19 |
| 20 | 21 | 22 | 23 | 24 | 25 | 26 |
| 27 | 28 | 29 | 30 | 31 |   |   |

## JUNE
| M | T | W | T | F | S | S |
|---|---|---|---|---|---|---|
|   |   |   |   |   | 1 | 2 |
| 3 | 4 | 5 | 6 | 7 | 8 | 9 |
| 10 | 11 | 12 | 13 | 14 | 15 | 16 |
| 17 | 18 | 19 | 20 | 21 | 22 | 23 |
| 24 | 25 | 26 | 27 | 28 | 29 | 30 |

## JULY
| M | T | W | T | F | S | S |
|---|---|---|---|---|---|---|
| 1 | 2 | 3 | 4 | 5 | 6 | 7 |
| 8 | 9 | 10 | 11 | 12 | 13 | 14 |
| 15 | 16 | 17 | 18 | 19 | 20 | 21 |
| 22 | 23 | 24 | 25 | 26 | 27 | 28 |
| 29 | 30 | 31 |   |   |   |   |

## AUGUST
| M | T | W | T | F | S | S |
|---|---|---|---|---|---|---|
|   |   |   | 1 | 2 | 3 | 4 |
| 5 | 6 | 7 | 8 | 9 | 10 | 11 |
| 12 | 13 | 14 | 15 | 16 | 17 | 18 |
| 19 | 20 | 21 | 22 | 23 | 24 | 25 |
| 26 | 27 | 28 | 29 | 30 | 31 |   |

## SEPTEMBER
| M | T | W | T | F | S | S |
|---|---|---|---|---|---|---|
|   |   |   |   |   |   | 1 |
| 2 | 3 | 4 | 5 | 6 | 7 | 8 |
| 9 | 10 | 11 | 12 | 13 | 14 | 15 |
| 16 | 17 | 18 | 19 | 20 | 21 | 22 |
| 23 | 24 | 25 | 26 | 27 | 28 | 29 |
| 30 |   |   |   |   |   |   |

## OCTOBER
| M | T | W | T | F | S | S |
|---|---|---|---|---|---|---|
|   | 1 | 2 | 3 | 4 | 5 | 6 |
| 7 | 8 | 9 | 10 | 11 | 12 | 13 |
| 14 | 15 | 16 | 17 | 18 | 19 | 20 |
| 21 | 22 | 23 | 24 | 25 | 26 | 27 |
| 28 | 29 | 30 | 31 |   |   |   |

## NOVEMBER
| M | T | W | T | F | S | S |
|---|---|---|---|---|---|---|
|   |   |   |   | 1 | 2 | 3 |
| 4 | 5 | 6 | 7 | 8 | 9 | 10 |
| 11 | 12 | 13 | 14 | 15 | 16 | 17 |
| 18 | 19 | 20 | 21 | 22 | 23 | 24 |
| 25 | 26 | 27 | 28 | 29 | 30 |   |

## DECEMBER
| M | T | W | T | F | S | S |
|---|---|---|---|---|---|---|
|   |   |   |   |   |   | 1 |
| 2 | 3 | 4 | 5 | 6 | 7 | 8 |
| 9 | 10 | 11 | 12 | 13 | 14 | 15 |
| 16 | 17 | 18 | 19 | 20 | 21 | 22 |
| 23 | 24 | 25 | 26 | 27 | 28 | 29 |
| 30 | 31 |   |   |   |   |   |

# ∾ 2014 ∾

## JANUARY
| M | T | W | T | F | S | S |
|---|---|---|---|---|---|---|
|   | 1 | 2 | 3 | 4 | 5 |   |
| 6 | 7 | 8 | 9 | 10 | 11 | 12 |
| 13 | 14 | 15 | 16 | 17 | 18 | 19 |
| 20 | 21 | 22 | 23 | 24 | 25 | 26 |
| 27 | 28 | 29 | 30 | 31 |   |   |

## FEBRUARY
| M | T | W | T | F | S | S |
|---|---|---|---|---|---|---|
|   |   |   |   |   | 1 | 2 |
| 3 | 4 | 5 | 6 | 7 | 8 | 9 |
| 10 | 11 | 12 | 13 | 14 | 15 | 16 |
| 17 | 18 | 19 | 20 | 21 | 22 | 23 |
| 24 | 25 | 26 | 27 | 28 |   |   |

## MARCH
| M | T | W | T | F | S | S |
|---|---|---|---|---|---|---|
|   |   |   |   |   | 1 | 2 |
| 3 | 4 | 5 | 6 | 7 | 8 | 9 |
| 10 | 11 | 12 | 13 | 14 | 15 | 16 |
| 17 | 18 | 19 | 20 | 21 | 22 | 23 |
| 24 | 25 | 26 | 27 | 28 | 29 | 30 |
| 31 |   |   |   |   |   |   |

## APRIL
| M | T | W | T | F | S | S |
|---|---|---|---|---|---|---|
|   | 1 | 2 | 3 | 4 | 5 | 6 |
| 7 | 8 | 9 | 10 | 11 | 12 | 13 |
| 14 | 15 | 16 | 17 | 18 | 19 | 20 |
| 21 | 22 | 23 | 24 | 25 | 26 | 27 |
| 28 | 29 | 30 |   |   |   |   |

## MAY
| M | T | W | T | F | S | S |
|---|---|---|---|---|---|---|
|   |   |   | 1 | 2 | 3 | 4 |
| 5 | 6 | 7 | 8 | 9 | 10 | 11 |
| 12 | 13 | 14 | 15 | 16 | 17 | 18 |
| 19 | 20 | 21 | 22 | 23 | 24 | 25 |
| 26 | 27 | 28 | 29 | 30 | 31 |   |

## JUNE
| M | T | W | T | F | S | S |
|---|---|---|---|---|---|---|
|   |   |   |   |   | 1 | 2 |
| 3 | 4 | 5 | 6 | 7 | 8 | 9 |
| 10 | 11 | 12 | 13 | 14 | 15 | 16 |
| 17 | 18 | 19 | 20 | 21 | 22 | 23 |
| 24 | 25 | 26 | 27 | 28 | 29 | 30 |

## JULY
| M | T | W | T | F | S | S |
|---|---|---|---|---|---|---|
| 1 | 2 | 3 | 4 | 5 | 6 | 7 |
| 8 | 9 | 10 | 11 | 12 | 13 | 14 |
| 15 | 16 | 17 | 18 | 19 | 20 | 21 |
| 22 | 23 | 24 | 25 | 26 | 27 | 28 |
| 29 | 30 | 31 |   |   |   |   |

## AUGUST
| M | T | W | T | F | S | S |
|---|---|---|---|---|---|---|
|   |   |   |   | 1 | 2 | 3 |
| 4 | 5 | 6 | 7 | 8 | 9 | 10 |
| 11 | 12 | 13 | 14 | 15 | 16 | 17 |
| 18 | 19 | 20 | 21 | 22 | 23 | 24 |
| 25 | 26 | 27 | 28 | 29 | 30 | 31 |

## SEPTEMBER
| M | T | W | T | F | S | S |
|---|---|---|---|---|---|---|
|   |   |   |   |   |   | 1 |
| 2 | 3 | 4 | 5 | 6 | 7 | 8 |
| 9 | 10 | 11 | 12 | 13 | 14 | 15 |
| 16 | 17 | 18 | 19 | 20 | 21 | 22 |
| 23 | 24 | 25 | 26 | 27 | 28 | 29 |
| 30 |   |   |   |   |   |   |

## OCTOBER
| M | T | W | T | F | S | S |
|---|---|---|---|---|---|---|
|   | 1 | 2 | 3 | 4 | 5 | 6 |
| 7 | 8 | 9 | 10 | 11 | 12 | 13 |
| 14 | 15 | 16 | 17 | 18 | 19 | 20 |
| 21 | 22 | 23 | 24 | 25 | 26 | 27 |
| 28 | 29 | 30 | 31 |   |   |   |

## NOVEMBER
| M | T | W | T | F | S | S |
|---|---|---|---|---|---|---|
|   |   |   |   | 1 | 2 | 3 |
| 4 | 5 | 6 | 7 | 8 | 9 | 10 |
| 11 | 12 | 13 | 14 | 15 | 16 | 17 |
| 18 | 19 | 20 | 21 | 22 | 23 | 24 |
| 25 | 26 | 27 | 28 | 29 | 30 |   |

## DECEMBER
| M | T | W | T | F | S | S |
|---|---|---|---|---|---|---|
|   |   |   |   |   |   | 1 |
| 2 | 3 | 4 | 5 | 6 | 7 | 8 |
| 9 | 10 | 11 | 12 | 13 | 14 | 15 |
| 16 | 17 | 18 | 19 | 20 | 21 | 22 |
| 23 | 24 | 25 | 26 | 27 | 28 | 29 |
| 30 | 31 |   |   |   |   |   |

# INTRODUCTION

The British Library's vast collections, spanning 30 centuries and representing nearly every country and language in the world, have been a marvellous treasure trove for this year's Diary.

Cats and dogs may not make the easiest of bedfellows but both species always have been close companions of man and so it is perhaps not surprising that they were illustrated quite often in medieval manuscripts, in oriental picture-books, on theatre posters, in children's ABCs and in many other publications. It may also not be very surprising that they are seldom depicted together! As you will see in this Diary, nearly all the illustrations here are of individual cats or dogs – for example, cats in witchcraft, cats in nursery rhymes (Ding Dong Bell) or fairy tales (Puss in Boots), and dogs in *The Hound of the Baskervilles* and *The Wonderful Wizard of Oz*. Many are by anonymous artists, but amongst those whose names we know are some wonderful illustrators, each with a very distinctive style – Gustave Doré, Aubrey Beardsley, Edward Lear, Randolph Caldecott, Cecil Aldin.

This is just a tiny fraction of the possible number of images that we could have selected. But we hope it gives you an idea of the great depth and range of the British Library's collections on almost any subject that you choose to research. Take a look at www.bl.uk. And come and visit us next time you are in London!

---

**31 MONDAY**

---

**1 TUESDAY**

New Year's Day
Holiday, UK, Republic of Ireland, USA, Canada,
Australia and New Zealand

---

**2 WEDNESDAY**

Holiday, Scotland and New Zealand

---

**3 THURSDAY**

---

**4 FRIDAY**

---

**5 SATURDAY**

Last Quarter

---

**6 SUNDAY**

Epiphany

---

'The Cat Who Walked by Himself'. Illustration from *Just So Stories* by Rudyard Kipling, 1902.
[12809.t.64]

omine ne m fu
oze tuo arguas
me neqz ut ira

7 MONDAY

8 TUESDAY

9 WEDNESDAY

10 THURSDAY

11 FRIDAY                                                                                          *New Moon*

12 SATURDAY

13 SUNDAY

David penitent with a harp and a dog, miniature from a Book of Hours, *c*.1460.
[Harley MS 5762, f.88]

# JANUARY

LEFT AND RIGHT: Illustrations by Walter Crane
from the *Golden Primer* by John Meiklejohn,
1884. [12805.w.33.]

14  MONDAY

15  TUESDAY

16  WEDNESDAY

17  THURSDAY

18 FRIDAY

*First Quarter*

19 SATURDAY

20 SUNDAY

# JANUARY

---

21 MONDAY                                    Holiday, USA (Martin Luther King's Birthday)

---

22 TUESDAY

---

23 WEDNESDAY

---

24 THURSDAY

---

25 FRIDAY

---

26 SATURDAY

---

27 SUNDAY                                                                    *Full Moon*

---

Illustration from *Under the Window* by Kate Greenaway, 1879.
[C.194.a.849]

Little boys and girls, will you come and ride
With me on my broomstick,—far and wide?
First round the sun, then round the moon,
And we'll light on the steeple, to hear a merry tune.

به سه مویی سر مکیسی به
شه این کل که وفا دار نیست
هر هنری طعنه شبی در
هر چراغ فلکیش ترنج
آنکه آرایش جان بنهاد درو
دیده فرو بسته اغیر خویش
در همه چیزی هنر و عیب هست
در سر طاق و گل رنگ بسی بست
بای بجایی جهان بعثت
گرک سگی بره و افتاده بود
بر سر آن جفت گروهی قطار

چون بدین ابن معنی بست آوری
هر علم جای و صد ا کنت
آتش صبحی در مطبخ
آنکه جاداری روی پر مرد
خانه بریشه زیبا برکه
دیده بریجت دکران کن قران
بتوان یافت بیش در چرا
یراغ کواربهدترین سیاه

بدود بنجا که بست آوری
هر گر آلوده صد صد کنت
نیم شماری زلف دردت
هم قدری لعم افزد کنت
موده کهی هیج بیسی نگار
صورت خود من بدروی بی غبر
ور دقص بوراز ابد بذبرباغ
دیده سپد است درو کون سیاه
به سیه بازی جیسی کنت
بوفص از ره مذرفتاده بود
نذکیکی آراو غوبض در چرا

ور به سر بون آمد جو چهیم
روی در ابمصلحت کنت
درو ۱۰۰ نجت بری
است در بوده اور رش
گسی واند صد بنیاد درکت
یکسکن و آیده عجب خوش
سرریس نامهزار آیده بدست
سبز پاس کجا در خوست

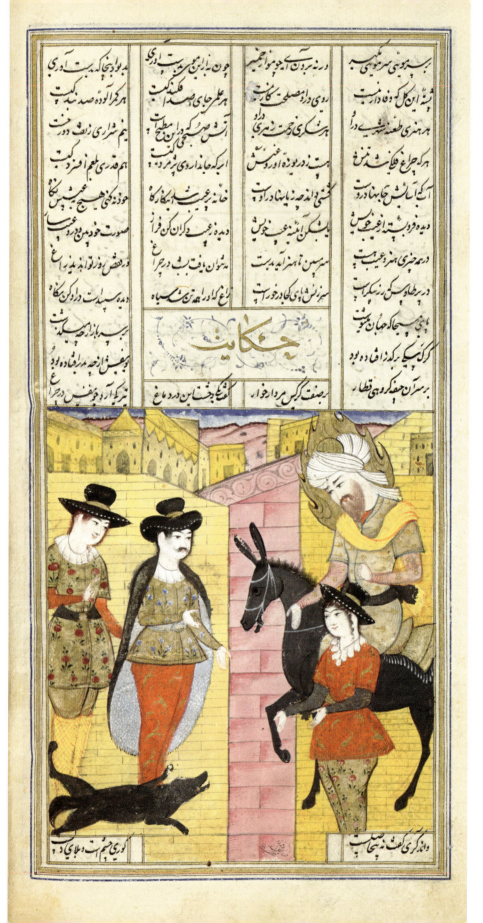

برصفت گرکس مرد ار خوار        کشته بخنابین درد ماغ

کوری جسم است و طلای د        واند کری کشت ز دیسناست

# JANUARY ·➤· FEBRUARY

**28 MONDAY**                                    Holiday, Australia (Australia Day)

**29 TUESDAY**

**30 WEDNESDAY**

**31 THURSDAY**

**1 FRIDAY**

**2 SATURDAY**

**3 SUNDAY**                                                        Last Quarter

'Jesus and the dead dog'. A miniature painting from a seventeenth century manuscript of Nizami's *Khamsa* ('*Five Poems*'), *c*.1665–67, Isfahan, Iran. [Add. MS 6613, f.19v]

# FEBRUARY

**4** MONDAY

**5** TUESDAY

**6** WEDNESDAY

Accession of Queen Elizabeth II
Holiday, New Zealand (Waitangi Day)

**7** THURSDAY

**8** FRIDAY

Illustration from *The Comic Adventures of Old Mother Hubbard and her Dog*, 1806.
[Ch.800/101]

## 9 SATURDAY

## 10 SUNDAY

*New Moon*
Chinese New Year

# FEBRUARY

---

11 MONDAY

---

12 TUESDAY                                                    Shrove Tuesday

---

13 WEDNESDAY                                                  Ash Wednesday

---

14 THURSDAY                                                St. Valentine's Day

---

15 FRIDAY

---

16 SATURDAY

---

17 SUNDAY                                                       First Quarter

---

'Dog guarding the Treasure' in *The Steadfast Tin Soldier* by Hans Christian Andersen, 1916.
Illustration by Harry Clarke. [K.T.C.102.a.15]

# FEBRUARY

---

**18 MONDAY**

---

**19 TUESDAY**

---

**20 WEDNESDAY**

---

**21 THURSDAY**

---

**22 FRIDAY**

---

**23 SATURDAY**

---

**24 SUNDAY**

---

Illustration from *The Historie of Foure-Footed Beasts describing the true and lively Figure of every Beast...* by Edward Topsell, 1607. [444.i.4]

# FEBRUARY ⤙ MARCH

25 MONDAY

26 TUESDAY

27 WEDNESDAY

28 THURSDAY

**1  FRIDAY**                    St. David's Day

**2  SATURDAY**

**3  SUNDAY**

LEFT AND RIGHT: 'The House that Jack Built' from *The Prince of Nursery Playmates*, 1885. [1869.a.22]

# MARCH

4  MONDAY                                                      *Last Quarter*

5  TUESDAY

6  WEDNESDAY

7  THURSDAY

8  FRIDAY

9  SATURDAY

10  SUNDAY                                                   Mother's Day, UK

Illustration by W.W. Denslow from *The Wonderful Wizard of Oz* by Frank L. Baum, 1903.
[12809.t.71]

*" You ought to be ashamed of yourself!"*

# MARCH

## 11 MONDAY

## 12 TUESDAY

## 13 WEDNESDAY

## 14 THURSDAY

## 15 FRIDAY

## 16 SATURDAY

## 17 SUNDAY

St. Patrick's Day
Holiday, Republic of Ireland

A young prince kneeling before a mullah, with scribal materials and a cat, miniature from *Dara Shikoh*, 1630–40. [Add. Or. MS 3129, f.18]

# MARCH

18 Monday

19 Tuesday
*First Quarter*

20 Wednesday
Vernal Equinox, (Spring begins)

21 Thursday

22 FRIDAY

---

23 SATURDAY

---

24 SUNDAY                                          Palm Sunday

Drawings by Henriette Ronner, 1895.
[7875.r.6]

# MARCH

## 25 MONDAY

## 26 TUESDAY

First day of Passover (Pesach)

## 27 WEDNESDAY

*Full Moon*

## 28 THURSDAY

Maundy Thursday

## 29 FRIDAY

Good Friday
Holiday, UK, Canada, Australia and New Zealand

A witch, a cavalier and Prince Rupert's dog from: *A Dog's Elegy, or Rupert's tears for the late defeat at Marston-Moore, ... where his beloved dog, named Boy, was killed..*, 1644. [E.3.(17)]

## 30 SATURDAY

## 31 SUNDAY

THE CATS HAVE COME TO TEA.

1 MONDAY

Easter Monday
Holiday, UK (exc. Scotland), Republic of Ireland,
Australia and New Zealand

2 TUESDAY

3 WEDNESDAY

*Last Quarter*

4 THURSDAY

5 FRIDAY

6 SATURDAY

7 SUNDAY

'The Cats Have Come to Tea' from *Marigold Garden* by Kate Greenaway, 1885.
[C.194.a.849]

# APRIL

**8  MONDAY**

**9  TUESDAY**

**10  WEDNESDAY**                    *New Moon*

**11  THURSDAY**

12 FRIDAY

13 SATURDAY

14 SUNDAY

LEFT: ' December', miniature by Simon Bening from
a Book of Hours, France (Tours), *c.*1540.
[Add. MS 18855, f.108v]
RIGHT: 'Dives and Lazarus', Psalm 114 from
*Tilliot Hours,* France [Loire School], *c.*1500.
[Yates Thompson MS 5, f.70v]

15 MONDAY

16 TUESDAY

17 WEDNESDAY

18 THURSDAY
*First Quarter*

19 FRIDAY

20 SATURDAY

21 SUNDAY
Birthday of Queen Elizabeth II

Toto and Dorothy in the tornado, illustration by W.W. Denslow from *The Wonderful Wizard of Oz* by Frank L. Baum, 1903. [12809.t.71]

---

**22 MONDAY**

---

**23 TUESDAY**                                           St. George's Day

---

**24 WEDNESDAY**

---

**25 THURSDAY**                                              *Full Moon*
Holiday, Australia and New Zealand (Anzac Day)

---

**26 FRIDAY**

---

**27 SATURDAY**

---

**28 SUNDAY**

---

'The Black Cat' by Edgar Allan Poe. Illustration by Aubrey Beardsley, 1845.
[Cup.820.bb.11]

# APRIL ·· MAY

## 29 MONDAY

## 30 TUESDAY

## 1 WEDNESDAY

## 2 THURSDAY

*Last Quarter*

## 3 FRIDAY

'The Cat and the Mouse' from *The Prince of Nursery Playmates*, 1885.
[1869.a.22]

4 SATURDAY

5 SUNDAY

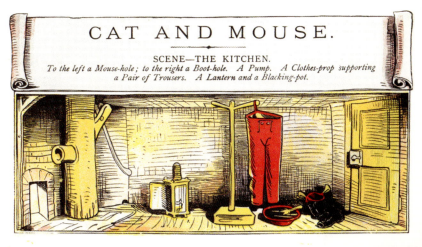

## CAT AND MOUSE.

SCENE—THE KITCHEN.

*To the left a Mouse-hole; to the right a Boot-hole. A Pump. A Clothes-prop supporting a Pair of Trousers. A Lantern and a Blacking-pot.*

A MOUSE her way towards the lantern wends,
To make a quiet meal off candle-ends,

But Pussy sees—springs—jumps—and then, alas!
She misses Tiny, but she breaks the glass.

7

6 MONDAY

Early Spring Bank Holiday, UK and Republic of Ireland
Holiday, Australia (Labour Day)

7 TUESDAY

8 WEDNESDAY

9 THURSDAY

Ascension Day

10 FRIDAY

*New Moon*

11 SATURDAY

12 SUNDAY

Mother's Day, USA, Canada,
Australia and New Zealand

'Mickey' from *Dogs of Character* by Cecil Aldin, 1927.
[7295.i.32]

# MAY

**13 MONDAY**

**14 TUESDAY**

A droite, à gauche, il va jetant
Sa griffe qu'il tient toute prête.
LIV. 1, FABLE VI.

**15 WEDNESDAY**     Feast of Weeks (Shavuot)

**16 THURSDAY**

17 FRIDAY

18 SATURDAY

*First Quarter*
Armed Forces Day, UK and USA

19 SUNDAY

Whit Sunday

LEFT: Fable VI from Fables of Florian, illustrated by
J.J. Grandville, 1842. [11483.i.58]
RIGHT: Fable XVII from Fables of Florian,
illustrated by J.J. Grandville, 1842. [11483.i.58]

Un soir en discutant (des docteurs c'est l'usage)
Ils comparaient entre eux les peuples anciens.
**LIVRE III, FABLE XVII.**

# MAY

21 TUESDAY

22 WEDNESDAY

23 THURSDAY

24 FRIDAY

Image from *Ehon kyoka yama mata yama*, 'Picture-book of Kyoka: Mountains upon Mountains'. A kyoka anthology illustrated by Hokusai, 1804. [16099.c.59.(1)]

25 SATURDAY

*Full Moon*

26 SUNDAY

Trinity Sunday

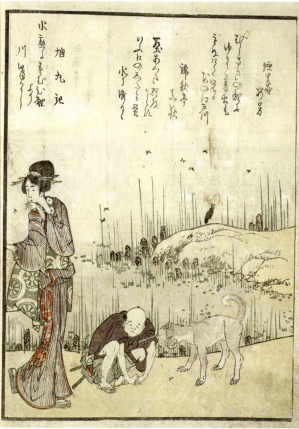

VIVE·LE·NOBLE·ROY·HENRY

# MAY ··· JUNE

**27 MONDAY**

Spring Bank Holiday, UK
Holiday, USA (Memorial Day)

**28 TUESDAY**

**29 WEDNESDAY**

**30 THURSDAY**

Corpus Christi

**31 FRIDAY**

*Last Quarter*

**1 SATURDAY**

**2 SUNDAY**

Coronation Day

The royal arms of England of Henry VII supported by a white greyhound and a red dragon.
[Royal MS 19 B. XVI, f.1v]

3 MONDAY

Holiday, Republic of Ireland
Holiday, New Zealand (The Queen's Birthday)

4 TUESDAY

5 WEDNESDAY

6 THURSDAY

7 FRIDAY

8 SATURDAY

*New Moon*
The Queen's Official Birthday (subject to confirmation)

9 SUNDAY

'Puss in Boots' pantomime poster, Drury Lane, 1885.
[Evanion 1903]

AUGUSTUS HARRIS'S
PANTOMIME.
PUSS IN BOOTS
DRURY LANE.
C. J. CULLIFORD & SONS, 2A FIELD COURT, LONDON.

# JUNE

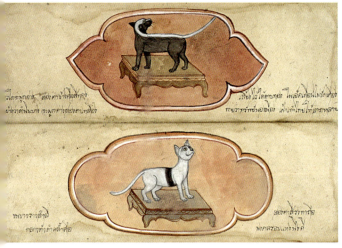

Holiday, Australia
(The Queen's Birthday),
subject to confirmation

Illustrations from a Thai treatise on Cats, second half
of the 19th century. [Or. MS 16797]

13 THURSDAY

14 FRIDAY

15 SATURDAY

16 SUNDAY

*First Quarter*
Father's Day, UK, Canada and USA

# JUNE

17 MONDAY

18 TUESDAY

19 WEDNESDAY

20 THURSDAY

21 FRIDAY                                    Summer Solstice (Summer begins)

'Basses and Contraltos' from *The Cecil Aldin Painting Book*, 1915.
[1871.B.25]

22 SATURDAY

23 SUNDAY                                                                          *Full Moon*

**BASSES**

**CONTRALTOS**

You see below, this funny Cat
Is playing music, while each Rat
Goes dancing round the Pussy's
stool,
Like children at a dancing school.

# JUNE

24 MONDAY

25 TUESDAY

26 WEDNESDAY

27 THURSDAY

28 FRIDAY

29 SATURDAY

30 SUNDAY                                                    *Last Quarter*

Illustration from *Pussie Cat's ABC book*, 1880.
[12805.n.30]

# JULY

1 MONDAY                                    Holiday, Canada (Canada Day)

2 TUESDAY

3 WEDNESDAY

4 THURSDAY                                  Holiday, USA (Independence Day)

5 FRIDAY

'Hey Diddle Diddle' from *The Hey Diddle Diddle Picture Book* by Randolph Caldecott, 1883.
[12805.r.53]

6  SATURDAY

7  SUNDAY

# JULY

---

8 MONDAY

---

9 TUESDAY

First day of Ramadân

---

10 WEDNESDAY

---

11 THURSDAY

---

12 FRIDAY

Holiday, Northern Ireland (Battle of the Boyne)

---

13 SATURDAY

---

14 SUNDAY

---

'Puss in Boots', frontispiece illustration by Gustave Doré from *Les Contes de Perrault*, 1862. [1871.f.11]

# JULY

### 15 MONDAY

St. Swithin's Day

### 16 TUESDAY

*First Quarter*

### 17 WEDNESDAY

Repos indispensable et bien acquis.

### 18 THURSDAY

19 FRIDAY

20 SATURDAY

Talents d'agrément.

21 SUNDAY

LEFT AND RIGHT: Illustrations from a French edition of *Dame Trot's Cat (Adventures de Dame Trot)*, 1858. [12808.a.15]

# JULY

*Full Moon*

---

23 TUESDAY

---

24 WEDNESDAY

---

25 THURSDAY

---

26 FRIDAY

---

Illustration from *Marigold Garden* by Kate Greenaway, 1885.
[C.194.a.849]

27 SATURDAY

28 SUNDAY

Am Brunnen stand ein großer Hund,
Trank Waſſer dort mit ſeinem Mund.
Da mit der Peitſch' herzu ſich ſchlich
Der bitterböſe Friederich;
Und ſchlug den Hund, der heulte ſehr,
Und trat und ſchlug ihn immer mehr.
Da biß der Hund ihn in das Bein,
Recht tief bis in das Blut hinein.
Der bitterböſe Friederich,
Der ſchrie und weinte bitterlich. —
Jedoch nach Hauſe lief der Hund
Und trug die Peitſche in dem Mund.

# JULY ⋅⋅ AUGUST

**29** MONDAY                                                                 *Last Quarter*

**30** TUESDAY

**31** WEDNESDAY

**1** THURSDAY

**2** FRIDAY

**3** SATURDAY

**4** SUNDAY

'The Story of Frederick' from *Der Struwwelpeter, oder lustige Geschichten und drollige Bilder für Kinder* by Heinrich Hoffman, 1876. [12839.i.13]

# AUGUST

5 MONDAY

Summer Bank Holiday, Scotland
Holiday, Republic of Ireland

6 TUESDAY

*New Moon*

7 WEDNESDAY

Eid-al-Fitr (end of Ramadân)

8 THURSDAY

9 FRIDAY

10 SATURDAY

11 SUNDAY

Illustration from *The Twins*, Cecil Aldin, 1910.
[1874.b.52]

# AUGUST

12 MONDAY

13 TUESDAY

14 WEDNESDAY                                        *First Quarter*

15 THURSDAY

16 FRIDAY

17 SATURDAY

18 SUNDAY

'The Boy Who Drew Cats' from *Japanese Fairy Tales* by Lafcadio Hearn, 1905. [11095.a.20]

# AUGUST

**19  MONDAY**

**20  TUESDAY**

**21  WEDNESDAY**                                                                *Full Moon*

**22  THURSDAY**

**23  FRIDAY**

Calendar page for May from a Book of Hours, Germany, early 16th century.
[Egerton MS 1146, f.5v]

24 SATURDAY

25 SUNDAY

AN UNINVITED GUEST

# AUGUST ⚬⚬ SEPTEMBER

**26** MONDAY                                    Summer Bank Holiday, UK (exc. Scotland)

**27** TUESDAY

**28** WEDNESDAY                                                      *Last Quarter*

**29** THURSDAY

**30** FRIDAY

**31** SATURDAY

**1** SUNDAY

Illustration by Cecil Aldin from *My Tabby Book*, 1923.
[YK.1996.b.9199]

# SEPTEMBER

**2  MONDAY**

Holiday, USA (Labor Day)
Holiday, Canada (Labour Day)

**3  TUESDAY**

**4  WEDNESDAY**

**5  THURSDAY**

*New Moon*
Jewish New Year (Rosh Hashanah)

**6  FRIDAY**

Constellations of Monoceros the Unicorn, Canis Major and Canis Minor from *A Celestial Atlas* by Alexander Jamieson, 1822. [533.g.31]

7  SATURDAY

8  SUNDAY

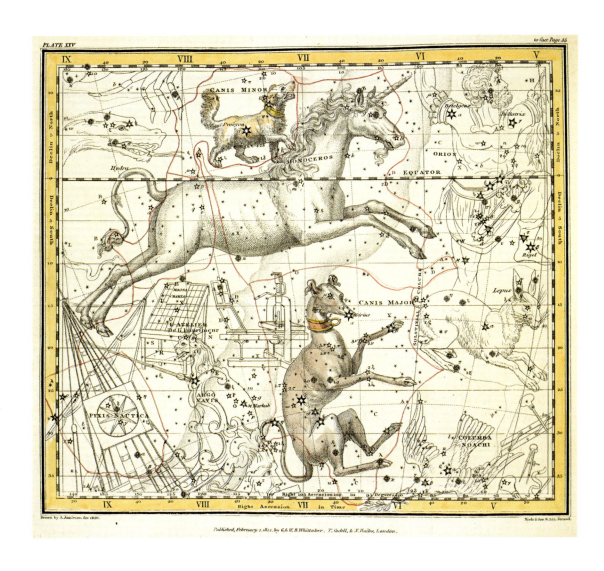

# SEPTEMBER

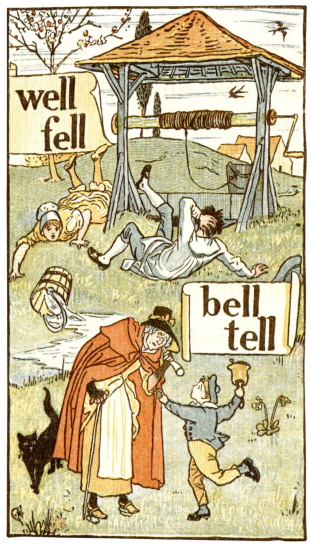

LEFT AND RIGHT: Illustrations by Walter Crane
from the *Golden Primer* by John Meiklejohn, 1884.
[12805.w.33.]

9 MONDAY

10 TUESDAY

11 WEDNESDAY

12 THURSDAY                    *First Quarter*

13 FRIDAY

14 SATURDAY          Day of Atonement
                     (Yom Kippur)

15 SUNDAY

# Hans Andersen's Fairy Tales

# SEPTEMBER

16 MONDAY

17 TUESDAY

18 WEDNESDAY

19 THURSDAY

*Full Moon*
First day of Tabernacles (Succoth)

20 FRIDAY

21 SATURDAY

22 SUNDAY

Autumnal Equinox (Autumn begins)

---

'Dog guarding the Treasure' in *The Steadfast Tin Soldier* by Hans Christian Andersen, illustrated by
E.J. Andrews and S. Jacobs, 1902. [12809.s.4]

# SEPTEMBER

**23**  MONDAY

**24**  TUESDAY

**25**  WEDNESDAY

**26**  THURSDAY

**27**  FRIDAY

*Last Quarter*

Dick Whittington releases his cat from a basket to chase away rats, from *Whittington and his Cat*, London, *c*.1845. [012806.ee.8]

28  SATURDAY

29  SUNDAY                                    Michaelmas Day

# SEPTEMBER ·•· OCTOBER

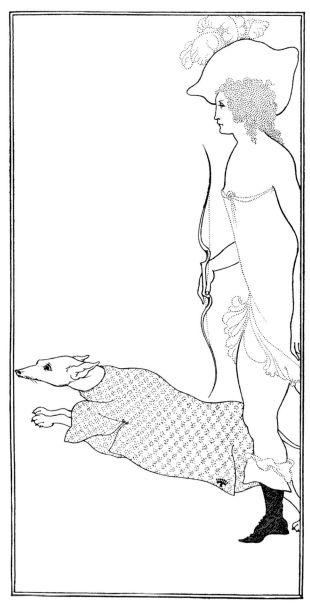

'Atalanta' from *A Book of Fifty Drawings* by
Aubrey Beardsley, 1897. [K.T.C.37.b.16]

30 MONDAY

1 TUESDAY

2 WEDNESDAY

3 THURSDAY

4  FRIDAY

5  SATURDAY                                                *New Moon*

6  SUNDAY

# OCTOBER

7 MONDAY

8 TUESDAY

9 WEDNESDAY

10 THURSDAY

11 FRIDAY                                                                 *First Quarter*

12 SATURDAY

13 SUNDAY

Miniature from a Book of Hours, France, *c.*1407.
[Add. MS 29433, f.20]

# OCTOBER

There was a Young Lady of Ryde, whose shoe-strings were seldom untied;
She purchased some clogs, and some small spotty Dogs,
And frequently walked about Ryde.

There was an Old Man of Kamschatka, who possessed a remarkably fat Cur;
His gait and his waddle were held as a model
To all the fat dogs in Kamschatka.

There was an Old Man of Leghorn, the smallest that ever was born;
But quickly snapt up he was once by a Puppy,
Who devoured that Old Man of Leghorn.

Limericks from *A Book of Nonsense* by
Edward Lear, 1885. [12332.dd.21]

14 MONDAY    Holiday, USA (Columbus Day)
Holiday, Canada (Thanksgiving)

15 TUESDAY

16 WEDNESDAY

17 THURSDAY

18 FRIDAY *Full Moon*

19 SATURDAY

20 SUNDAY

"THE HOUND OF THE BASKERVILLES."

(*See page* 252.)

# OCTOBER

## 21 MONDAY

## 22 TUESDAY

## 23 WEDNESDAY

## 24 THURSDAY

United Nations Day

## 25 FRIDAY

## 26 SATURDAY

*Last Quarter*

## 27 SUNDAY

British Summer Time ends

Sir Arthur Conan Doyle's *Hound of the Baskervilles*, Sidney Paget illustration from *The Strand Magazine*, August 1901–02. [PP.6004.glk]

# OCTOBER ·· NOVEMBER

---

28 MONDAY

Holiday, Republic of Ireland
Holiday, New Zealand (Labour Day)

---

29 TUESDAY

---

30 WEDNESDAY

---

31 THURSDAY

Halloween

---

1 FRIDAY

All Saints' Day

---

2 SATURDAY

---

3 SUNDAY

*New Moon*

---

'There was an Old Woman who Rode on a Broom' from *Old King Cole's Book of Nursery Rhymes*,
illustrated by Byam Shaw, 1901. [X.992/4798]

# NOVEMBER

4 MONDAY

5 TUESDAY

Guy Fawkes<br>Islamic New Year begins (subject to sighting of the moon)

6 WEDNESDAY

7 THURSDAY

8 FRIDAY

'Alice and the Duchess' from Lewis Carroll's *Nursery Alice*, illustration by Sir John Tenniel, 1890.
[Cup.410.g.74]

9  SATURDAY

10  SUNDAY

*First Quarter*
Remembrance Sunday

# NOVEMBER

**11 MONDAY**

Holiday, USA (Veterans Day)
Holiday, Canada (Remembrance Day)

**12 TUESDAY**

**13 WEDNESDAY**

**14 THURSDAY**

15  FRIDAY

16  SATURDAY

17  SUNDAY

Illustrations from *A Detection of damnable driftes, practized by three Witches araigned at Chelmisforde in Essex, ..., whiche were executed in Aprill. 1579, etc.*, 1579. [C.27.a.8]

SCOTLAND

A correct outline
of
Scotland
by
Lilian Lancaster
designer of
Geographical Fun

# NOVEMBER

18  MONDAY

19  TUESDAY

20  WEDNESDAY

21  THURSDAY

22  FRIDAY

23  SATURDAY

24  SUNDAY

Map of Scotland as Dick Whittington and his Cat, drawn by Lilian Lancaster, 1869.
[Maps CC.5.a.223]

# NOVEMBER ·– DECEMBER

## 25 MONDAY

*Last Quarter*

## 26 TUESDAY

## 27 WEDNESDAY

Hannukah begins

## 28 THURSDAY

Holiday, USA (Thanksgiving Day)

## 29 FRIDAY

'Ding Dong Bell' from *The ABC of Nursery Rhymes*, 1892.
[12806.l.61]

## 30 SATURDAY

St. Andrew's Day

## 1 SUNDAY

First Sunday in Advent

Curly Locks? Curly Locks?
Wilt thou be mine?
Thou shalt not wash dishes
Nor yet feed the swine
But sit on a cushion
And sew a fine seam
And feed upon strawberries
Sugar and cream.

Ding dong bell Pussy's in the well.
Who put her in? Little Tommy Lin
Who pulled her out? Little Tommy Trout
What a naughty boy was that
To drown poor Pussy-cat.

# DECEMBER

2 MONDAY

3 TUESDAY                                                                              *New Moon*

4 WEDNESDAY

5 THURSDAY

6 FRIDAY

7 SATURDAY

8 SUNDAY

Illustration from *The Twins* by Cecil Aldin, 1910.
[1874.b.52]

# DECEMBER

9 MONDAY *First Quarter*

10 TUESDAY

11 WEDNESDAY

12 THURSDAY

13 FRIDAY

14 SATURDAY

15 SUNDAY

Dog and Partridges, miniature from
a Bestiary, England, *c*.1230–40.
[Harley MS 4751, f.48]

16 MONDAY

17 TUESDAY

*Full Moon*

18 WEDNESDAY

19 THURSDAY

20 FRIDAY

21 SATURDAY

Winter Solstice (Winter begins)

22 SUNDAY

'Hey Diddle Diddle', from *Mother Goose*, 1913. Illustration by Arthur Rackham.
[11646.h.32]

# DECEMBER

THE OWL AND THE PUSSY-CAT.

I.

THE Owl and the Pussy-Cat went to sea
In a beautiful pea-green boat,
They took some honey, and plenty of money,
Wrapped up in a five-pound note.
The Owl looked up to the stars above,
And sang to a small guitar,
"O lovely Pussy ! O Pussy, my love,
What a beautiful Pussy you are,
You are,
You are !
What a beautiful Pussy you are !"

'The Owl and the Pussycat', illustration from
*The Nonsense Book* by Edward Lear, 1910.
[12812.bb.26]

23 MONDAY

24 TUESDAY                    Christmas Eve

25 WEDNESDAY                  Christmas Day
Holiday, UK, Republic of
Ireland, USA, Canada,
Australia and New Zealand

26 THURSDAY                   Boxing Day
Holiday, UK, Republic of
Ireland, Canada, Australia
and New Zealand

## 27 FRIDAY

## 28 SATURDAY

## 29 SUNDAY

172    SYLVIE AND BRUNO.

came forwards to meet them, keeping his musket pointed straight at Bruno, who stood quite still, though he turned pale and kept tight hold of Sylvie's hand, while the Sentinel walked solemnly round and round them, and looked at them from all points of view.

"Oobooh, hooh boohooyah!" He growled at last. "Woobah yahwah oobooh! Bow wahbah woobooyah? Bow wow?" he asked Bruno, severely.

'A Visit to Dog Land' from *Sylvie and Bruno* by Lewis Carroll, 1889. Illustration by Harry Furniss. [12807.t.26]

# DECEMBER ·•· JANUARY

---

**30 MONDAY**

---

**31 TUESDAY**

New Year's Eve

---

**1 WEDNESDAY**

New Year's Day
Holiday, UK, Republic of Ireland, USA,
Canada, Australia and New Zealand

---

**2 THURSDAY**

Holiday, Scotland and New Zealand

---

**3 FRIDAY**

---

**4 SATURDAY**

---

**5 SUNDAY**

---

'The Dear Little Puppy' from Lewis Carroll's *Nursery Alice*. Illustration by Sir John Tenniel, 1890.
[Cup.410.g.74]

6 MONDAY

7 TUESDAY

8 WEDNESDAY

9 THURSDAY

10 FRIDAY

11 SATURDAY

12 SUNDAY

Illustration from *The White Kitten Book* by
Cecil Aldin, 1909. [12034.w.14]